THE PLACE OF WORSHIP

Pastoral Directory on the Building and Reordering of Churches

VERITAS

IRISH INSTITUTE OF PASTORAL LITURGY

The first edition of this Directory was published
in 1966.

A second edition was published in 1972 and this
third edition (1991) has been considerably revised
and expanded.

Published in this format by Veritas Publications and
the Irish Institute of Pastoral Liturgy 1994

Copyright © 1994 Irish Episcopal Commission
for Liturgy

Design: David Cooke

Printed in the Republic of Ireland

ISBN 1 85390 272 1

CONTENTS

ABBREVIATIONS

ADVISORY SERVICE

The Advisory Committee on Sacred Art and Architecture welcomes requests for advice as to the interpretation of, or application of, the Directory to particular cases. When an architect has been appointed the request should be made through him or her. In all cases enquiries should be addressed to:

> The Honorary Secretary
> Advisory Committee on Sacred Art and Architecture
> Irish Institute of Pastoral Liturgy
> College Street
> Carlow

ACKNOWLEDGEMENT

The Irish Episcopal Commission for Liturgy acknowledges the contribution of the Advisory Committee on Sacred Art and Architecture and other consultors.

Members of the Advisory Committee include:

> Most Revd Joseph Duffy, Bishop of Clogher (Chairman)
> Ray Carroll, Artist
> Revd Seán Collins, OFM
> Revd Robert Harrison
> Richard Hurley, Dip Arch, FRIAI
> Revd Patrick Jones
> John Kernan, B Arch, FRIAI
> Laurence McConville, DA, ARIBA
> Revd Patrick McGoldrick
> Very Revd Timothy O'Connor, PP
> Paul J. O'Daly, Dip Arch, MRIAI
> Revd Henry O'Shea, OSB
> Rt Revd Mgr Seán Swayne, PP
> Michael Wynne, MSA, STL, PhD

ILLUSTRATIONS

The illustrations in this Directory are from the Christian Celtic period and are reproduced by kind permission of the Office of Public Works (pp. 7, 13, 15, 22, 23, 29, 35, 39, 45, 46 & 48), National Museum of Ireland (pp. 11, 19, 21, 25, 31, 40, 42 & 43) and the Board of Trinity College, Dublin (pp. 9, 26 & 28).

INTRODUCTION

This Directory has been prepared to meet the practical needs of clergy, parish committees, architects, artists, contractors and all those involved in the construction and refurbishment of church buildings. The approach is as comprehensive as a manageable reference book will allow: full account is taken of those who are coming to a major project for the first time and also of those in charge of churches who need to keep their thinking in line with current liturgical developments.

The Directory contains basic information but always with an eye on the liturgical assembly, the ministers and people who actually use or will use the building. For this reason it spells out a vision of faith which explains the information and unifies the various stages of the planning and execution. The vision is of God gathering his people together and being present among them. He makes his people holy and they in turn give him praise through prayer and the offering of their lives. He tells his people about himself and about the Christian life to which he has called them and which they have already begun to live. Like any other building a church is a piece of architecture, the result of human intelligence and skills applied to various materials. But it differs from other buildings in that it is first and last a work of faith and a sign of faith. It is a sign of a world redeemed in Christ and filled with the Spirit of God, and yet a world in which the fruits of redemption have still to be fully recognised and won. This vision of faith runs like a silver thread through the Directory. It is the vision of the Constitution on the Liturgy of the Second Vatican Council, which set in motion a total reform of the liturgy of the Catholic Church. It is the same vision which one finds in the introduction to the Roman Missal which we now use at Mass. And because of its fidelity to this vision, the Directory is more than a manual: it is an important instrument of education. It brings home to us the basic task of preparing priests and people to undertake liturgical improvements, especially in the layout and furnishing of churches. Those parishes which have already taken up the challenge appreciate the experience - the pain and the enrichment, the labour and the reward of the process. Pastorally, the task has to do with spiritual formation and growth, with building up a faith which is informed, active and community-based. The gesture of a short retreat, or at least a period of recollection, for a building team, including the parish committee, puts down the initial markers in their proper place. The Directory invites reflection and discussion. It does not, unfortunately, eliminate the pain; nor does it provide a standard solution for all projects. But it points the way forward with vigour and clarity. The predecessor of this Directory appeared in 1972. Since then the level of liturgical awareness has been rising steadily all the time. Reflection and experience have taught us many lessons. The revised Directory aims at a presentation of church architecture which understands more deeply the principles of Vatican II and expresses more fully its vision. The vision remains the same. There is no attempt here, as there was no attempt in the earlier Directory, to prescribe any particular form of architecture, as public opinion tended to do so often in the past. Cultivating a suitable style demands openness to changing cultural patterns as well as respect for continuity with the past. The Directory recognises fully the careful consideration which the choice of style requires but resolutely refuses to take sides. It is more concerned with the conviction that what makes a church different from any other building is not its form or shape but rather how it facilitates for a particular community of believers a regular unfolding of the Christian mystery, the eternal divine plan for humanity as revealed in the person of Jesus Christ.

In a passage from the Old Testament which is frequently used in the dedication of churches, Solomon prays that the Lord would watch over his house, the Temple which he had built (1 KINGS 8:29). His prayer of faith in our day is expressed by all those priests and people who undertake the massive commitment to build or rebuild and who otherwise care lovingly for their churches. I have just made the point that a place of worship is basically different from other buildings. It calls for spiritual qualities on the part of those responsible for its construction and maintenance, qualities which go beyond technical skills and even artistic flair. They are the qualities which surface when a true sense of the liturgy has been achieved; reverence for the divine presence, devotion to its protection, trust in its permanence. They are the qualities which make their own the poetry of the great doxology:

> Through him,
> With him,
> In him,
> In the unity of the Holy Spirit,
> All glory and honour is yours,
> Almighty Father,
> Forever and ever.

So much for the church building in general. In effect, the weight of the following pages is taken up with the material elements and furnishing of the interior. As with the overall design of the building, the purpose is to ensure that the design of the elements serves their immediate function as well as conveying their relative significance. The need for guidance is most obvious with those elements which are also the major focal points of the liturgy. These are chiefly the altar, the chair, the ambo, the tabernacle, the baptismal font and the confessional. Of all the elements the altar has pride of place because it is the altar which defines the entire space of the church as the place of celebration for the eucharist. The tabernacle, on the other hand, is the place of reservation for the Blessed Sacrament when the celebrating is over. Its meaning and function, therefore, are different from those of the altar. While the altar is the focus of public worship, the tabernacle creates a haven of peace and quiet, a space of private adoration and prayer in the permanent living presence of the Lord. The Directory gives the relationship between the altar and the tabernacle special attention because it touches on a basic principle of liturgical renewal.

Every new house awaits the arrival of its inhabitants and is already a sign of the quality of their presence. Like any house used by people, a church also mediates presence, God's presence to us and our presence to him in response. In a human house we can be ourselves, we listen and we speak, we see one another and we acknowledge one another. In the house of God, we can also be ourselves, but in the deeper truth of his love. We listen to his saving word, we contemplate him, we are accepted by him. The inner personal concentration we achieve in our prayer is not to the exclusion of others. On the contrary, it informs all our external activities in church, our language, our music, our movements. It belongs both to the immediate purpose and the ultimate meaning of the church. It is our response to the mysterious presence in the deepest reaches of our being, to the Word which takes flesh in us as it has already taken flesh in the Lord Jesus. Finally, as one who has worked with the members of the Advisory Committee on Sacred Art and Architecture over the past six years, I am pleased to record my admiration and appreciation for their dedication, diligence and unfailing zest for this project.

Go gcúití Dia a saothar dóibh.

✠ Joseph Duffy
Bishop of Clogher

Chairman
Advisory Committee on Sacred Art and Architecture to the Irish Episcopal Commission for Liturgy

Feast of the Guardian Angels, 1993

1   CHURCH BUILDING AND THE LITURGICAL ASSEMBLY

The term 'church': its meaning and significance

1.1   A church building, in the official language of the Catholic Church, is a sacred building intended for divine worship to which the faithful have the right of access for the exercise, especially the public exercise, of divine worship (CIC 1214).

1.2   The church building must be seen both as the house of God and the house of the people of God.

It is the house of God in the sense that there God is present in his people, in his word, in the sacramental ministry and in the reserved Blessed Sacrament. It is also the house of the people of God, set aside for their celebration of the liturgy. There when the faithful assemble Christ is present and active through sacramental signs. There they gather as a Christian community to hear the word of God, to pray together, to celebrate the sacraments and to participate in the eucharist. There too they worship privately outside the liturgy.

Basic to an understanding of the nature and function of the church building is an understanding of the liturgical assembly.

The liturgical assembly

1.3   From the beginning the practice of assembling for worship was characteristic of the way of life of Christians. The first Christians saw themselves as a people, the people of God, in continuity with the Israelites whom God had called together and formed into a people under Moses (EXODUS 19-24). Spontaneously they organised themselves to worship as a people, particularly through their weekly assembly on Sundays. It was when they assembled that they were most conscious of themselves as a people and were most clearly identifiable as a people.

During the middle ages the concept of liturgical assembly, like the practice of the liturgical assembly, became somewhat eroded. Later the communal nature of Christian worship was obscured, and worship came to be looked upon largely as a private matter between the individual and God.

Happily, as a result of the Second Vatican Council, liturgy is seen once again as the communal worship of the entire assembly. It is the worship offered to the Father in the Spirit by the entire body of Christ, head and members.

Clarification of terms

1.4   The word 'church' corresponds to the Greek *ekklesia*, rendered in Latin as *ecclesia*, which originally denoted the local Christian community assembled for worship. Literally *ekklesia* means 'those called together' (by God). Later the word came to refer also to the building which housed those called together, the building where the assembly took place, the assembly-house.

MOSES, AARON AND HUR, CROSS OF MUIREDACH, MONASTERBOICE

2 THE MEANING OF THE LITURGICAL ASSEMBLY

2.1 The Christian assembly and its liturgy have a number of essential characteristics which need to be understood. In particular the designer needs to consider that:

A) The worshippers are a priestly people.

B) Within the worshipping assembly the priest has an essential role: to preside over the assembly in the person of Christ.

C) The entire assembly celebrates the liturgy.

D) Within the assembly there is a variety of functions.

E) Christ is present in every celebration of the liturgy.

F) The worshippers are a united people.

G) Liturgical celebration engages the whole person, body as well as spirit.

H) Liturgical celebrations should be characterised by reverence.

I) The spirit of the liturgical celebration is one of festivity.

J) In the liturgy heaven and earth are one.

K) In the liturgy the Christian community celebrates and fosters the victory of Christ in all those who in any way struggle to overcome self-seeking, enmity and indifference to others and strive to build a new society of concern and of peace on this earth.

A priestly people

2.2 The people who form the liturgical assembly, the baptised faithful, are a 'kingly and priestly people' (cf. 1 PETER 2:4-10). In baptism they receive a character which qualifies them for the priestly task of worship. Essentially this worship consists of the living out of a life pleasing to God (cf. ROMANS 12:1). But the priestly attitude underlying such a life will in turn seek ritual expression in the worship of the liturgy, the official worship of the Church.

Role of the priest

2.3 The priest presides over the assembly. He directs and leads the people's prayer. He prays, he performs sacred actions, he preaches the word, he leads the people in offering sacrifice, he breaks for them the bread of the eucharist. All this he does because at his ordination he received the priestly character by which he is empowered to act in the person of Christ.

The office of the ordained priest is indicated by the place and chair which he occupies, by the ministers who assist him, and by the marks of respect shown to him.

The entire assembly celebrates the liturgy

2.4 Since the entire assembly shares in the priesthood of Christ through baptism, the entire assembly celebrates the liturgy. Liturgical celebration is not the concern of the clergy only. Nor are the worshippers mere silent spectators. Rather, the celebration calls for the full and active involvement of the entire assembly. It is in this sense that one can say that the entire assembly celebrates, the entire assembly is celebrant.

Designing for liturgy therefore means designing

for a celebrating people, actively involved through word and song, through gesture and movement, through ceremonial and ministry - actively involved above all in heart and mind.

Variety of functions

2.5 While all in the assembly have an active part to play, not all have the same role. In addition to the ministry of presiding, a ministry most commonly carried out by the priest, there is a variety of other ministries, e.g. those of deacon, reader, cantor, all of whom have their own individual roles to fulfil. Hence the observation of the Roman Missal in relation to the eucharist:

> The people of God assembled at Mass reflects an organic and hierarchical arrangement, expressed by the various ministries and actions for each part of the celebrations (GIRM 257).

Christ's presence in every celebration

2.6 Jesus Christ promised to be with his followers until the end of time (MATTHEW 28:20). Even when 'two or three' gather in his name he is present in their midst (MATTHEW 18:20). This presence of the Lord is realised above all in the liturgy.

To assemble for worship, therefore, is to gather in the Holy Spirit around the person of Jesus Christ the Lord, risen, alive and glorious. Through him the faithful worship the Father in the Spirit.

In the celebrations of the eucharist the presence of the Lord is realised in four ways:

A) in the body of the faithful 'gathered' in his name;

B) in the word of God proclaimed in the assembly: when the scriptures are proclaimed in the liturgy Christ himself speaks to his faithful;

C) in the person of the priest, by whose ministry Christ both offers himself to the Father and reaches out to the assembled faithful;

d) finally and above all in the sacrament of his body and blood.

A united people

2.7 Through the death and resurrection of Christ, God's children, who in biblical terms were 'scattered' through sin and disbelief, have been gathered into one (JOHN 11:52), by one Spirit baptised into one Body (1 CORINTHIANS 12:13). Gathered for worship, therefore, they are bonded together in the Lord: united in their common belief in him, in their common commitment to him, in their common sharing in his life, in their common concern for his kingdom, in their common love for one another. In their worship 'the whole Body of the Church lifts its prayer up to heaven with a single heart' (SAINT JOHN CHRYSOSTOM).

In the liturgical assembly, therefore, there is 'neither Jew nor Greek' (GALATIANS 3:28), but a gathering which transcends differences of age, sex, colour or walk of life.

Nor can the assembly ever be elitist. It must remain open to all, saint and sinner alike.

In its worship the assembly is also conscious of its absent members and of its union with the Church throughout the world. Where the local Church is at worship, there is the universal Church. In every eucharist the entire Church offers, the entire Church is offered.

Worship engages the whole person, body and spirit

2.8 Worship is primarily internal, but not exclusively so.

It has its bodily dimension too, engaging participants in the totality of their being, body as well as spirit. People engaged in worship not only will and think; they speak and sing, play and dance, move and celebrate. And liturgy involves all these activities.

Worship too has its material dimension. It has to do with nature, with the material world through which we reach out to God and which proclaims to us God's presence and goodness. Liturgy uses such material elements as bread and wine, water and oil, fire and light; it requires symbol and ritual, and through them it creates the kind of environment which opens up people's capacity for worship and helps make their experience of worship an experience of prayer, an experience of God.

Reverence

2.9 Over the centuries Christian liturgy has always been characterised by a sense of reverence. The celebration of the liturgy is a celebration of sacred things. True, God is believed by Christians to be close to them - intimately close to them - as their Father, through Jesus Christ, in the Holy Spirit. But they believe that God is also Lord of the cosmos, the Lord of glory, the Lord of indescribable majesty. In the celebration of the liturgy, therefore, the believer's attitude is always one of reverence and awe, wonderment and love.

Accordingly liturgy and liturgical environment call for a climate of awe, mystery and wonder. Poorly designed furnishings, shoddy vestments, tawdry appointments and tasteless decor militate against such a climate and impede rather than facilitate good liturgical celebration.

A spirit of festivity

2.10 All liturgy is a celebration in joy of the wonderful things God has done through the life, passion and resurrection of Jesus Christ. All liturgy is a gathering around the person of Jesus Christ, risen and glorious, to join him in his worship of the Father. For these reasons the liturgy is festive. It is a victory celebration, the celebration of Christ's victory and of the victory of his followers over sin and death. Those who celebrate remember that 'we are an Easter people, and Alleluia is our song' (SAINT AUGUSTINE).

Heaven and earth are one in the liturgy

2.11 Ultimately there is only one liturgy, that which is being offered by the risen Lord to his Father in heaven. When the faithful celebrate the liturgy they somehow transcend the here and now and become part of that timeless worship of heaven. In our liturgical celebration, this one eternal liturgy breaks in upon us and we participate in this 'single chorus of praise' (SAINT JOHN CHRYSOSTOM). Because of our earthbound human condition, all this requires to be expressed and experienced in sign and symbol. Only in the life to come will the liturgy be celebrated in the blessed face-to-face vision of the Creator.

The challenge to designers

2.12 From the foregoing it is obvious that the challenge to all involved in liturgical design is to create the kind of environment which will reflect and articulate the nature of the Christian assembly and its liturgy. Space and light, materials and furnishings, suitable places for the various liturgical activities, ambiance and atmosphere - all must combine to help Christians become what they are when they worship: a priestly people gathered in the joy of the Holy Spirit around the risen Lord, worshipping the Father in body as well as in spirit and caught up in the timeless worship of heaven.

3 BUILDING AND REORDERING OF CHURCHES: GUIDING PRINCIPLES

Suitability for active participation

3.1   In building or reordering a church one must take as one's major guiding principle the church's suitability for the full and active participation of the entire assembly in the liturgy. Furthermore the entire worship space and its furnishings should be designed so as to foster prayer and reflect the holiness of the sacred mysteries (cf. GIRM 253-254).

In building or reordering a church one must take as one's major guiding principle the church's suitability for the full and active participation of the entire assembly in the liturgy. Furthermore the entire worship space and its furnishings should be designed so as to foster prayer and reflect the holiness of the sacred mysteries (cf. GIRM 253-254).

If this is to be achieved, fidelity to high artistic standards will be required in accordance with Chapter 4 below, and the buildings and requisites for worship as signs and symbols of heavenly things should be truly worthy and beautiful.

All of this must be seen as part of liturgical renewal, the whole aim of which is 'the full and active participation by all the people' in the liturgy (SC 14).

Planning for participation

3.2   The overall plan should be inspired by the aim of facilitating optimum participation on the part of the assembly, both verbal and auditory, both bodily and spiritual. This will require careful placing of the assembly, provision for adequate movement and an arrangement in which the individual will be aware that he or she is part of the full community of ministers and people. It will also require effective visibility, acoustics, illumination, heating and ventilation.

The many forms of liturgy

3.3   While the church will be designed primarily for the Sunday celebration of the eucharist, it must also provide for the proper celebration of other liturgical functions such as eucharist on weekdays, baptism and the other sacraments, prayer services, especially morning and evening prayer, and funerals.

Sanctuary not designed in isolation

3.4   Within the overall design the sanctuary should not be considered in isolation from the rest of the building. Rather the building should be considered as a whole, in the light of the principles of liturgical celebration set out above. Accordingly the relationship between all parts of the church, together with the various technical factors involved, should be taken into account and a master plan prepared, even though financial or social considerations may require that the work be carried out in stages.

Simplicity

3.5   The architecture and decoration should be marked by a noble simplicity (GIRM 287). Simplicity does not imply impoverishment, and the authentic expression of the Christian virtue of poverty can give powerful witness in the face of the increasing materialism of modern life.

Welcoming atmosphere

3.6   The atmosphere of the church should be welcoming, with minimum physical or psychological barriers to participation in the liturgy.

Architectural style

3.7 The Church has not adopted any particular style in relation to church art and architecture. In fact it insists that the art of our own time be given free scope in church, provided it accords with the reverence due to the sacred buildings and rites (SC 123).

Role of the artist

3.8 All the liturgical elements in the church, as well as images and shrines, should be designed by artists and the work coordinated by the architect. This applies especially to the more important elements such as the altar, chair, ambo, baptismal font and tabernacle. For fuller discussion of the role of the artist see Chapter 4.

Appointment of artists

3.9 It is desirable that the appointment of artists take place at the earliest possible stage. A good working relationship between artist, architect and client will help to ensure the unity of harmony and design which is so necessary to the success of a church building project.

Principles for new and existing buildings

3.10 The principles set out in this Directory apply equally to both new and existing places of worship.

4 ART IN THE SERVICE OF THE LITURGY

4.1 Architects and artists give glory to God through their work. They communicate something of their intuition of the divine and through their imagination give some insight into the mysteries of faith, which are inaccessible to reason alone.

Function of the architect and artist

4.2 The function of the architect and artist, working with their respective skills and experience, is to

A) create an environment which will facilitate and encourage liturgical celebration;

B) give expression in visual terms to aspects of doctrine and of spirituality which cannot be adequately expressed in words alone;

C) establish relationships between the liturgical elements which will emphasise their specific character and clarify the connections between them.

It is not the task of the architect and artist merely to decorate buildings or to provide devotional images, although such services are part of their true task.

The Church always presses into her service the arts cultivated by the various nations and wishes to give them a place in its worship. While preserving artistic treasures of former times and adapting them to current needs it also encourages new developments in the arts (GIRM 254).

The power of art

4.3 Because of the power of art to touch the emotions and the sub-conscious, artists can exercise an enormous influence for good if the statements made by their work are in harmony with the faith of the Church. Every work is either a reflection of its initial creator, God, or a distortion of that reflection.

Christian art

4.4 Sacred art must strive to offer us a visual synthesis of all the dimensions of our faith. Church art must aim at speaking the language of the incarnation, and through material things express the One who 'deigned to dwell in matter and bring about our salvation through matter, according to Saint John Damascene's beautiful teaching' (DS 11).

4.5 The place of the artist can never be taken by the craftsperson or by the provider of 'religious' goods. Art builds upon craft, giving to merely practical objects a quality of transcendence that links the material and the spiritual world. The work of the artist is not a superfluous luxury.

Requirements in the artist

4.6   It should be noted that the ability to draw, carve or sculpt does not make an artist, although such skills are essential. In addition the artist needs to have an understanding of the nature and purpose of the liturgy, a sensitive approach to the character of the subject matter and a sympathy with the needs and problems of the faithful who will use or will be influenced by the work in question.

Commercial artefacts

4.7   It is unsatisfactory to furnish a church or any part of it with ready-made artefacts that come from commercial providers. Such an approach would in effect constitute a failure to engage in the creative effort which is necessary in order to find what is uniquely appropriate in each particular instance.

Works of art

4.8   Art is the servant of the liturgy. Works of art, which include the liturgical furnishings and other objects used in worship, are part of the environment of the church and should take account of the renewed emphasis on participation by the liturgical assembly. Works which distract from or militate against the worship of the liturgical assembly are unsuitable and out of place.

4.9   The authentic work of art excludes everything that is false, cheap or shoddy, pretentious or superficial. Accordingly, objects marked by mediocrity or lack of artistic merit are specifically excluded from the church (SC 124).

> The world in which we live has need of beauty in order not to lose hope. Beauty, like truth, fills the heart with joy, and this thanks to your hands! (MESSAGE OF THE FATHERS OF THE SECOND VATICAN COUNCIL TO ARTISTS, 8 DECEMBER 1965)

Styles of art

4.10   Since the Church adopts no particular style of art

as its own (SC 123), artists are guaranteed the artistic liberty they need (GS 62). For their part they should cultivate a true sense of religion and liturgy. They should also respect the need for some recognisable representation in images in order that they may help to establish a sense of the presence of God in those who need such a visual stimulus.

Materials and creative ability

4.11   A wide variety of materials may be considered for use by the artist: tapestry, paint and enamel, as well as sculpture in wood, stone, fibreglass, metal, etc.

4.12   Where familiar symbols are used, care should be taken that they are not presented in a lifeless, archaeological manner. Nor is the skilful execution of contemporary idioms sufficient. What is needed is creative flair on the part of a committed and theologically informed artist.

The use of ornament

4.13   Ornament can be an effective means of enhancing the setting of the liturgy, and so of facilitating fuller participation in it. Its purpose is to express more clearly the structural forms of a building, and the function and relative importance of the various spaces within the building.

4.14   Ornament of a permanent nature should be a development of the form or structure of the building, and it should be the work of an artist or designer of quality. Ornament of an ephemeral nature, such as flowers, candles and banners, ought to be treated likewise with sensitivity and control. Ornament should serve and enhance the liturgical and devotional functions of the space. Side chapels, shrines or any other part of a church should not be so adorned as to draw emphasis away from the sanctuary.

4.15   The use of ornament expresses a spirit of generosity in the service of the liturgy. It implies sacrifice in spending talents, energies and material resources so as to give thanks and glory to God. And this is fully consonant with the Christian spirit of poverty.

5   CLIENT, ARCHITECT AND ARTIST

Primary authority

5.1   Primary authority and responsibility for the nature and quality of the church building rests with the Ordinary, who is generally the diocesan bishop (SC 124, CIC 134, 834i, 838i). The client is the person who acts on behalf of the Ordinary and who will have the advice and support of the relevant commissions of the diocese or religious institution or other community (SC 44, 45, 46).

Importance of cooperation

5.2   The success of a church building project depends more on the cooperation between client and architect than on any other single factor. The greatest care should therefore be exercised in the selection of the client/ design team so as to achieve the best results.

Choosing architect and artist

5.3   The final choice of the architect rests with the Ordinary, following consultation with the client and the diocesan commission. Because so much depends on the wisdom of this choice, a decision should be made only after much study of the merits of possible candidates. The final choice of architect will often be determined by the excellence of work already done. Among other measures for arriving at a suitable choice the client might consider commissioning an independent architect to prepare a report on the relevant facts which should be considered in the selection of the architect and other experts for the project and in the preparation of the design brief.

5.4   The choice of artists should be made by the client on the advice of the architect and in consultation with the relevant commissions of the diocese. This choice requires the same serious considerations as that of the architect. It is particularly important that there should be a good working relationship between architect and artists so that a unity and harmony in design concept may be established and maintained. It is desirable that the appointment of artists be made at the earliest possible stage.

5.5   For a successful working relationship between client, architect and artists it is essential that each should have a sympathetic appreciation of the aims of the others in the design and construction of the church and a real confidence in their integrity.

The design brief

5.6   A fundamental requirement for the success of a project is the preparation jointly by client and architect, in consultation with the relevant diocesan commissions, of a design brief*, which is a process for defining and analysing the relevant facts and

---

* *A more detailed statement of the function of the diocesan commissions and of the possible*

the design problems. It is the task of the architect to provide a creative solution to the problems which have been identified. Adequate funds should be made available to enable the requirements of the brief to be fulfilled.

---

content of design briefs and outlines of management procedures for controlling the design and construction process may be found in a document entitled Diocesan Commissions for Sacred Art and Architecture published by the Advisory Committee on Sacred Art and Architecture to the Episcopal Commission for Liturgy on 21 November 1975 (See THE FURROW Vol 27 (1976) 308-316 & 504-510).

Ongoing cooperation

5.7 Cooperation between client and architect should continue throughout the entire project until the completion of the building in order to ensure that the design concepts are fulfilled and that the technical aspects are dealt with effectively.

5.8 Cooperation between client and architect should extend to every aspect of the design of a church and its furnishings, even to such matters as advice on the choice of vestments.

6 ENVIRONMENT OF THE CHURCH

The church:
place of prayer and sign of prayer

6.1 The design of the church should indicate its unique character, differentiating it from buildings of a purely secular nature. It stands not only as a place of prayer but as a sign of prayer, a sign too of the pilgrim Church or people of God on earth. At the same time it reflects the heavenly Church, the assembly of the blessed in heaven (ODEA 2: 1-2).

6.2 The church building should also reflect the traditions and history of the area and people. Careful study should be made of the environmental conditions so as to ensure that the building is sensitively related to the spirit and topography of the location.

Environment: underlying principles

6.3 In order to establish the most suitable environment the following principles should be considered:

A) The building should be integrated into its surroundings and location, whether this be urban, suburban or rural. Open spaces which are desolate and depressing and which discourage visits to the church should be avoided.

B) The immediate vicinity of the church should be capable of providing for open-air liturgical celebrations such as the lighting of the paschal fire at the Easter Vigil and the procession on Palm Sunday or on other major feast days.

C) Access to the church should be made as easy as possible. This is primarily a matter of avoiding psychological as well as physical barriers.

D) There should be a clear relationship with and access to the presbytery, social centre, hall, schools and other subsidiary facilities.

E) There should be a transitional space leading to the internal recollected space of the church and reflecting the relationship between the secular activities of daily life and the spiritual activities of worship.

Parking and access

6.4 Parking areas should be to the back or at least to the side of the church and should always be landscaped, through the use of trees and shrubs, through variations of levels and of surface pavings, etc., in such a manner that vehicles are concealed as much as possible and a shelter belt is provided against wind and storms.

6.5 Access to the main door of the church should be provided for funeral hearses, ambulances, wedding cars, etc.

7 THE ENTRANCE AREA

(Place of Welcome)

Design, form and significance

7.1   On entering the church one comes into the welcoming presence of the Lord. The entrance therefore should be inviting in character and human in scale so that people will feel at home in the Lord's house.

The location and design of the entrance should be such that the passer-by is encouraged to enter and pray.

7.2   The entrance could take one of many forms, including some development of the traditional atrium and ambulatory.

7.3   The design of the entrance should express the essential unity of liturgy and life by providing a visual relationship between the sacred and the secular. It should encourage an attitude of recollection and calm.

7.4   The entrance has a particular significance in relation to baptism, the first step in our entrance or initiation into the people of God. Here the baptism of children or the admission of catechumens normally begins, since baptism is 'the door to life and to the kingdom of God' (GICI 3).

7.5   The practice in some situations of people remaining in the entrance during the liturgy should be discouraged by attention to the design of this area.

Function of the entrance area

7.6   The entrance should be able to cater for various activities relating to the pastoral life of the community.

For this reason the main entrance area should be more than a mere draught lobby. It should be large enough to provide for a reasonable gathering space and for a worthy entrance into the church. It should be adequately insulated from external noise.

7.7   Another service which the entrance provides is to accommodate the paschal fire and at least some of the participants at the Easter Vigil, in situations where the fire cannot be lighted outside the church.

Paschal fire base

7.8   Where, on the other hand, it is possible to have the paschal fire outside the church a generous space should be provided for it. Within that space it would be desirable to provide a permanent location and base for the fire as an ongoing reminder of the Easter Vigil and of Christ's triumph over sin and death.

Holy water fonts

7.9   It is desirable to have one or more holy water fonts at the entrance. These should be generous in size and inviting in form (e.g. an open bowl). The use of metal dispensers is neither a worthy nor a fitting way to treat this sacramental.

Shrines at entrance

7.10   The entrance area could incorporate one or more shrines or images of the saints, particularly of the titular saint of the church. It could also serve to display and accommodate objects relating to the history of the church and its location (Cf. Chapter 20, Images in the Church).

Subsidiary porches and other facilities

7.11 Subsidiary porches should be limited to the number required for reasons of public safety and practical necessity. If they are likely to be used frequently they should meet the minimum criteria set out above.

7.12 Facilities should also be provided for related activities such as the sale of books, for a notice-board of adequate size, and for the particular needs of local groups.

7.13 At least one entrance should be able to cater for wheelchairs, with sufficiently wide doors and handles of a kind suitable for the disabled. Any steps should be equipped with suitable handrails.

7.14 If a sound amplification system is provided in the church it would be desirable to include a microphone socket outlet in the entrance area so that liturgical celebrations there will be audible to people inside the church.

7.15 From the entrance area the toilet facilities of the church should be easily identifiable.

ST MOLAISE'S BOOK SHRINE, DETAIL

8 THE PLACE OF ASSEMBLY

Designing the worship space as a whole

8.1 From the nature of the liturgical assembly as discussed above (chapters 1 and 2) it follows that

A) the faithful worship not as so many individuals but rather as a single people gathered in unity;

B) the presiding celebrant and other assistants, while having a special role to fulfil, remain part of the assembly.

All this should be reflected in the design of the worship space as a whole and in the manner in which the altar and other liturgical elements are integrated into that space. For a discussion of the sanctuary see below, Chapter 11.

Places for the faithful

8.2 The places for the faithful should be planned so as to facilitate their full, conscious and active participation (SC 14 & GIRM 273). They should be able to see and hear easily, and the entire arrangement should help them become 'one body, hearing the word of God, joining in prayer and song, and offering sacrifice and sharing the Lord's table together' (GIRM 62).

8.3 Full participation cannot be achieved when the congregation is too far removed from the focus of liturgical action.

Seating

8.4 Seating should be flexible and capable of being arranged so as to suit the various needs of different kinds of assemblies, especially on particular occasions. Since the traditional bench seating tends towards the regimentation of the assembly and the curtailing of easy movement and active participation, alternatives should be considered. Moreover, the elimination of bench seating (e.g. by the use of chairs) would make it possible to cater for different activities in the church while at the same time maintaining the relevant safety arrangements. If however some bench seating is to be retained it should be so designed as to appear as inconspicuous as possible and to cause the least possible hindrance to movement for the congregation.

8.5 The layout should facilitate a dignified and orderly movement at holy communion.

Provision for choir and musicians

8.6 The design of the church should include a special place for the choir. The choir should be located in such a way that it is clearly seen to be part of the assembled community, and that it can carry out its ministry effectively, viz. leading and sustaining the congregational singing as well as performing its own proper parts. The location of the choir should also facilitate the full participation of its members in the liturgy.

8.7 The pipe organ is to be held in high esteem in the Latin Church, for it is the traditional instrument which adds a wonderful splendour to the Church's ceremonies, and powerfully lifts people's minds to God and to higher things (SC 120).

A pipe organ should be planned for all new churches, even if it cannot be installed immediately.

8.8 It is highly advisable in the initial stages of work on a church to seek guidance from the organ builder and the music director. The location of the choir should take into account the location of the organ console, the position of the director of singing and of the cantor, and the need to avoid any unnecessary distraction to the assembly.

8.9 Accommodation should also be provided for other types of music. This would involve sufficient space for a small orchestra, adequate power supplies, and microphone sockets for electronic instruments.

8.10 Space should be provided for a movable lectern for use by leaders of singing, commentators and those making announcements. This space should be in full view of all, but not in the sanctuary area.

Table for gifts

8.11 A special place should be determined for a table from which the gifts are carried in procession to the altar in the course of Mass. The table should be located so that the procession will pass through the congregation and thus highlight the participation of all the faithful in the eucharist.

Dedication crosses

8.12 It is praiseworthy to keep the ancient custom of placing crosses made of stone, brass or other suitable material or having the crosses carved on the walls of the church. Thus twelve or four crosses should be provided according to the number of anointings and suitably distributed on the walls of the church at a convenient height. A small bracket should be fitted beneath each cross, into which is fixed a small candlestick with a candle to be lighted (ODEA 2:22).

Other uses of the church

8.13 Subject to the approval of the Ordinary, churches can sometimes be used for functions other than worship. Provision should be made when designing the church for the showing of slides, video-recordings and films, for the indirect projection of images, for special lighting and sound effects, and for the operation of cameras and sound-recorders.

ST MANCHAN'S SHRINE, DETAIL

9 THE PLACE OF PREPARATION

(Sacristy/Vestry)

The sacristy

9.1 Liturgy demands preparation. This in turn demands a preparation area with certain facilities; this is called the sacristy.

9.2 The purpose of the sacristy is to provide for the storage and preparation of the sacred vessels, liturgical books and vestments. The sacristy may be used by the priest for vesting and for prayer before and after the liturgy, although these activities can with advantage be carried out in the main body of the church.

9.3 The location of the sacristy and any subsidiary spaces should be such as to facilitate the organisation of processions at the beginning and end of the liturgy. The location should also be such that priests and people can easily meet one another. In general a location near to and directly off the main entrance will be most suitable.

Other facilities

9.4 Provision might be made for

A) a vesting room for acolytes and lay ministers;

B) an office for interviews with parishioners and for the administration of parish records;

C) a workroom convenient to the sanctuary for the storage, maintenance and cleaning of equipment, the arrangement of flowers and the preparation of the thurible;

D) a storeroom for fittings and furnishings which are not in regular use;

E) toilet facilities for priests and ministers;

F) facilities for individuals who may become indisposed during a liturgical celebration.

9.5 The proper storage of objects which can easily be damaged by dust, e.g. vestments and altar linen, should be given special care.

CALL OF ST MATTHEW (?), CROSS OF THE SCRIPTURES, CLONMACNOIS

10 THE PROCESSIONAL WAYS

10.1 Processions have been traditional in the Church from earliest times. They take place for a variety of reasons:

A) to provide formal entrances and recessions on the occasion of liturgical celebrations;

B) to enhance the celebration of the eucharist
– at the carrying of the Gospel book as a sign of reverence;
– at the presentation of the gifts as a sign of the people's participation;
– at communion time as a sign of the spiritual union of the communicants;

C) in association with certain rites, e.g. marriage (at the entrance and exit of the bridal party) and funerals (at the reception of the body in the church);

D) as events in their own right, e.g. the Corpus Christi procession;

E) on the occasion of the celebration of baptism, when people may process from door to ambo, from ambo to font and from font to altar;

F) as a public expression of witness, penitence, praise or supplication.

Sometimes processions evoke the great biblical themes of exodus and journey, and remind the participants that here on earth they are a pilgrim people.

Processional routes

10.2 Wide routes should be provided so that processions can be carried out in a dignified manner. This applies especially in relation to the communion procession. The principal processional route is from the main entrance of the church towards the sanctuary.

10.3 The layout of the processional ways should facilitate easy access by the congregation, including disabled persons, to all locations within the church.

APOSTLES/BISHOPS, NORTH CROSS, AHENNY

11 THE SANCTUARY

Integration of the sanctuary into the entire worship space

11.1 The sanctuary is that part of the church in which the central action of the liturgy takes place. It is distinguished by the elements it contains and the activities which relate to them. The principal elements are

– the chair, marking the place of presidency
– the ambo, from where the word of God is proclaimed
– the altar, centre of the eucharistic banquet/sacrifice.

11.2 The relationship of the sanctuary to the entire worship space should be such that the whole assembly is clearly seen to be a single priestly community, actively involved in worship, even though structured by a variety of ministries (those of bishop, priest, deacon, choir, cantor, reader, acolyte, minister of the eucharist, commentator, etc.).

For this reason the sanctuary, in structure and decoration, should be integrated into the entire complex.

Design of the sanctuary

11.3 The sanctuary should be spacious enough to allow for dignified movement of the ministers. In the celebration of the eucharist, for example, the movement of the priest is in the following order:

– from sacristy in procession (preferably through the assembly) to the altar, which is then reverenced
– from altar to chair for the introductory rites

– from chair to ambo for the liturgy of the word (if necessary)
– from ambo (or chair) to altar for the liturgy of the eucharist
– from altar to communion station for the distribution of communion
– finally, from communion station back to altar or chair for the concluding rites.

In designing these routes it should be kept in mind that the priest may be accompanied in some of these movements by ministers.

11.4 The space surrounding each element should also be such that when a liturgical activity is taking place the element in use emerges as the focal point of attention.

11.5 In designing the sanctuary the elements should be considered together, both in relation to one another and in relation to the elements outside the sanctuary, e.g. baptistry or tabernacle (the latter is not an essential sanctuary element: cf. Chapter 16, The Place of Reservation). The theological significance of all these elements and their liturgical function should be clearly defined.

11.6 The place of sacramental communion or communion station requires no special element but must nevertheless be a clearly defined place facilitating the communion procession in addition to the distribution of communion.

If the place of reservation (tabernacle) is located within the sanctuary it should accord with the principles indicated in Chapter 16 below.

11.7 Whenever a higher floor level is used for the sanctuary this level should be to whatever height is required for adequate vision on the part of the entire assembly, but not to a height which would impose a spatial or psychological barrier between sanctuary and congregation.

Images

11.8 If images such as paintings or statues are to be placed in a church, in accordance with the directives given in Chapter 20, they should be located where they will not distract from the liturgical action, and therefore outside the sanctuary. On the other hand, images which relate directly to the liturgy may be appropriate in the sanctuary, provided they form an integral part of the architectural concept and do not clutter or confuse the space.

STOWE MISSAL SHRINE, DETAIL.

12 THE PLACE OF PRESIDENCY

(The Chair)

The presidential chair

12.1 The priest presiding over the liturgy does so 'in the person of Christ'. Through the words, gestures and person of the priest Christ reaches out to his people, leading them in the worship of the Father. Gathering for worship is gathering around Christ present in the priest.

12.2 The office of liturgical presidency is expressed by the president's chair. The chair marks the place of presidency and is the focal point of the attention of the faithful at the opening of the liturgical celebration.

12.3 A worthy place of presidency with a well designed chair can heighten the people's awareness of the presence and role of Christ in the liturgy. Even outside the celebration the chair can be evocative of this presence and role.

12.4 The chair should be the work of an artist, and such as to underline its significance. At the same time it should not be remote or dominant or throne-like; the priest, though presiding over the assembly, is himself a member of the assembly, is in fact its servant.

Design and location

12.5 In its design the chair should harmonise with the other sanctuary elements.

12.6 The location of the chair should

A) allow the chair itself and the priest when seated to be clearly visible to the assembly;

B) be architecturally defined, e.g. by the use of a platform or a different floor finish, or by relating it to some feature of the building such as a column or arch;

C) be planned in relation both to the chair's function and to the other elements in the church;

D) enable the priest to preside from it effectively;

E) permit all activities to take place normally in front of it. This means that it is preferable that neither ambo nor altar be placed behind or in a line with the chair.

Use of the chair

12.7 The chair therefore is not merely a convenient place to which the priest can retire when the focus of attention is on the ministry of others in the assembly. During the eucharist, for example, the priest at the chair actively participates in the following ways:

A) He greets the people from the chair, thereby expressing the presence of the Lord in the assembled community.

B) He conducts and joins in the penitential rite.

C) He leads the people in singing or reciting the Gloria.

D) He invites the people to pray in silence, and then he says the Opening Prayer.

E) He listens with prayerful attention to the word of God.

F) He preaches the homily (alternatively he may do so from the ambo).

G) He leads the people in the profession of faith.

H) He directs the prayer of the faithful.

I) He may join the people in silent prayer after communion.

J) He says the Prayer after Communion.

K) Finally, he greets the people, imparts his blessing, and sends them forth 'to do good works, praising and blessing the Lord' (GIRM 57).

Alternatively, he may carry out these last three activities from the altar.

Unnecessary additions

12.8 The unique character of the chair should not be obscured by placing other objects near it. For example, there is no need for a lectern or bookstand at or near the chair; an acolyte can easily hold the book for the few moments required. Additional unnecessary furniture tends to distract from the main elements.

Seats for ministers

12.9 'The seats for the ministers should be located in the sanctuary in places convenient for their functions' (GIRM 271), and they should not suggest either through their design or their location that the ministers share in the presidential role of the priest.

The bishop's chair or 'cathedra'

12.10 The ministry of presidency outlined above is symbolised pre-eminently in the chair or cathedra of the bishop, since he is the high-priest and teacher of his diocese, presiding over its whole life in the name of Christ. The chair for the priest-celebrant should be set up in a place separate from that of the bishop's chair (CB 47).

13 THE PLACE OF THE WORD

(The Ambo)

BEGINNING OF ST MATTHEW'S GOSPEL, DETAIL, BOOK OF KELLS

Ambo and lectern

13.1 'The dignity of the word of God requires the church to have a suitable place for announcing his message so that the attention of the people may be easily directed to that place during the liturgy of the word' (GIRM 272). This place is the ambo with its reading desk or 'lectern', and from it is proclaimed the word of God in the scripture readings and responsorial psalm, and the Easter Vigil Exsultet. It may also be used for the homily and the prayer of the faithful.

Purpose of the ambo

13.2 The ambo is much more than merely a place from which to read. It is the table of the bread of the word, just as the altar is the table of the bread of the eucharist. When the scriptures are proclaimed in the liturgy, Christ himself is speaking to his faithful and they are celebrating his presence in the word. The ambo then is the place from which the word of God is proclaimed with its power to touch the hearts and lives of the hearers (ISAIAH 55:10-11; ROMANS 1:16; HEBREWS 4:12).

13.3 The ambo should be reserved for those who proclaim the word and sing the psalm. It is less fitting for others to use the ambo, e.g. a cantor leading the singing, commentator or person making announcements. If necessary, these should use rather a simple movable stand which must in no way compete visually with the ambo or distract from the liturgy (see also Chapter 8.10).

Design and location

13.4 The ambo in design and location should

A) normally be permanent;

B) enable the minister to be easily seen and heard by the assembly;

C) be large enough to accommodate on occasion several ministers, e.g. priest or deacon with thurifer and acolytes;

D) even when not in use be a clear reminder of the dignity of the word of God;

E) have any microphones which may be necessary as unobtrusive as possible;

F) accommodate any necessary light fittings while respecting the integrity of the lectern;

G) have the lectern of fixed height and angle rather than adjustable;

H) not normally have a shelf, but if one is required it should be concealed;

I) be at an adequate distance from the president's chair and altar to allow for dignified movement whether of one person or of a group.

Ambo in chapels, oratories and prayer rooms

13.5 Chapels, oratories and prayer rooms should contain an ambo unless space does not allow for an adequate one.

Display of the gospel book

13.6 The practice of displaying the gospel book permanently in the church is recommended, and in the design of the church consideration should be given to the provision of a suitable place for it.

14 THE PLACE OF EUCHARIST

(Altar of Sacrifice, Table of Sacred Banquet)

Altar, the focal point

14.1 The Christian altar is by its very nature both altar of sacrifice and table of the sacred banquet.

14.2 It is the altar of sacrifice where the sacred mysteries are celebrated under sacred signs. It is also the table of banquet around which the faithful assemble to give thanks or eucharist to God and to share in the supper of the Lord.

14.3 The altar is therefore the focal point of the church and the centre of the eucharistic celebration, the great act of thanksgiving. It is also the focal point around which the Church's other rites are in a certain manner arranged (cf. ODEA 4:4 & GIRM 259, 262).

Design and significance

14.4 The altar should be designed and treated with the greatest reverence. And since it is at the altar that the memorial of the Lord is celebrated and his body and blood given to the people, it is seen traditionally as a sign of Christ himself, a silent yet eloquent witness to his saving work which is perpetuated throughout the ages until he comes again. This is why the tradition of the Church can say: 'The altar is Christ'.

14.5 Consequently the altar must be pre-eminent in every respect: in its location as the focal point of the assembly (though not necessarily in a spatial sense); in the quality of its material; in the beauty and skill of its design and workmanship, and in the manner in which it expresses the sacred mysteries. For these rea-

LOAVES AND FISHES, CROSS OF MOONE

sons the service of an artist is necessary.

14.6 Because of its significance the physical integrity of the altar should be respected. The altar should never be cut or drilled to receive or hold extraneous objects, e.g. microphone sockets, cables, brackets or hangings.

One altar only

14.7 There should be only one altar in a church. In the assembly of the people of God the one altar signifies the one Saviour Jesus Christ and the one eucharist of the Church. However, a separate weekday Mass chapel may also contain its own altar (ODEA 4:7).

Fixed and movable altars

14.8 It is desirable that in every church there should be a fixed altar, i.e. an altar attached to the floor so that it is not movable, and that in other places set aside for sacred worship there should be either a fixed or a movable altar (ODEA 4:6).

Free-standing

14.9 The altar should be free-standing, catering for Mass facing the people and capable of being encircled by the priest and other ministers.

14.10 In the case of the reordering of a church it must be emphasised that the mere moving forward of the table of an existing altar while leaving the tabernacle set in an existing reredos almost never provides a proper solution. The reordering of a sanctuary for liturgical celebration has to do with much more than making provision for Mass facing the people. It calls also for the reordering of many elements, especially altar, ambo, chair and tabernacle in such a way as to facilitate good liturgical celebration (cf. Chapter 27.7–9).

Materials

14.11 In accordance with the received custom of the Church and the biblical symbolism associated with the altar, the table of a fixed altar should be of stone, indeed natural stone. However, any fitting, solid and skilfully constructed material may be used (ODEA 4:9).

14.12 A movable altar may be made from any material which is solid and dignified, suitable for liturgical use (GIRM 264).

Size of the altar

14.13 There is no uniform size for the altar. Nor does a large space necessarily demand a large altar. What is important is its design. Even in a large building a small altar can still dominate the space by reason of the power and dynamic quality of its design - a result which can be obtained by an informed and skilled artist.

The size of the altar is not related to or affected by concelebration. Concelebrants do not stand at the altar but 'around it in such a way that the people are able to see the rite clearly. The concelebrants should remain out of the way of the deacon when he ministers at the altar' (GIRM 167).

Altar appointments

14.14 Altar appointments should be subordinate to the altar itself in design and scale. The altar must never be used as a table of convenience for leaflets, cruets, notes or anything of a similar nature. On it should rest only the bread, the wine and the book. Candles may be placed on the altar provided they do not block the view. A cross too may be placed on the altar. (Alternatively candles and/or cross may be placed near the altar.) If flowers are to be placed on the altar they should be few and should not diminish the integrity and symbolism of the altar.

14.15 Since the altar is a symbol of Christ, it should not be obscured by superfluous objects when the liturgy is not being celebrated, and all such things (bookstands, books, candlesticks, flowers, microphone, etc.) should be removed immediately the celebration has finished.

Elevation of the altar

14.16 The altar should be elevated sufficiently to facilitate adequate visibility on the part of the entire assembly. On the other hand it should not be so elevated as to become psychologically remote from the people.

Dedication and blessing; relics

14.17 Fixed altars are to be dedicated and movable ones either dedicated or blessed according to the prescribed rites. The ancient practice of placing relics of martyrs or of other saints beneath a fixed altar is to be retained in accordance with the prescribed rites (cf. CIC 1237).

In this connection the following should be noted:

A) Relics should be of such a size that they can be recognised as human; excessively small relics may not therefore be used.

B) Relics should be authentic; it is better to omit them altogether than to use relics of doubtful authenticity.

C) The reliquary is to be placed beneath the table of the altar as the design of the altar may allow, but not on or in the table.

D) It is not permitted to place relics in the base of a movable altar.

Images of saints over the altar

14.18 In new churches statues or pictures of saints may not be placed over the altar. Likewise relics of saints should not be placed on the table of the altar when they are being exposed for veneration (ODEA 4:10).

15 THE CROSS

The significance of the cross

15.1 'There should be a cross on the altar or near it, easily seen by the congregation' (GIRM 270).

15.2 The cross should call to mind the paschal mystery of Christ, that is his passion, his triumphant resurrection and his final coming in glory to which Christians look forward.

Like the altar itself the cross is a reminder of Christ's sacrifice, which is made sacramentally present and in which the faithful participate at the eucharist. The relationship between altar and cross should be reflected in their design.

Location

15.3 The cross should be located in such a way that it is clearly visible to the congregation and may easily be venerated and incensed.

It may be placed 'on the altar' according to the Roman Missal (GIRM 270). However, such an

RINNAGAN CRUCIFIXION PLAQUE

arrangement can cause problems since the cross must be large enough to be visible to the congregation without at the same time blocking their view of the ministers at the altar or of the gifts upon it.

Another arrangement is the standing cross which may also be used as a processional cross. Carried in the entrance procession the cross can evoke the coming of Christ among his assembled people as well as Christ leading his people on their earthly pilgrimage to the Father. (The processional cross should not be placed in the sanctuary if there is already a permanent cross there; in such a case it is placed out of sight when not being carried.)

Other alternatives are the suspended cross or the cross mounted on a wall or upright.

15.4 The cross should be so located that it does not obscure the action of the ministers or any feature of the church, and that it is not itself obscured by contrasting elements such as back lighting or stained glass windows.

16 THE PLACE OF RESERVATION

(The Tabernacle)

Purpose of reservation

16.1 The place of reservation relates to the ancient tradition of reserving the Blessed Sacrament when Mass is over. The purpose of this reservation is to provide for communion of the sick and for adoration, both public and private.

In designing for reservation it should be kept in mind that the eucharistic celebration itself is the true centre of the Church's worship, and indeed of the whole Christian life. The actual celebration of the eucharist is the focus of the normal Sunday assembly, and the altar its centre (see Chapter 14.3, The Place of Eucharist and EM 1).

Underlying principles

16.2 In providing for the reservation of the Blessed Sacrament the following should be kept in mind:

A)   in the reserved sacrament Christ is really present. Not only while the sacrifice is being offered and the sacrament received, but as long as the eucharist is kept in our churches and oratories Christ is truly Emmanuel, that is, 'God with us'; day and night he is in our midst, dwelling with us, full of grace and truth (MF 62). The reserved sacrament, therefore, is to be shown the veneration and adoration that is due to God himself, as has always been the practice recognised by the Catholic Church (ES 3)

B)   the reserved sacrament provides for the communion of those who are unable to participate in the eucharistic celebration, and for adoration. 'The primary and original reason for the reservation of the eucharist outside Mass is the administration of viaticum. The secondary ends are the giving of communion and the adoration of our Lord Jesus Christ present in the sacrament. The reservation of the sacrament for the sick led to the praiseworthy practice of adoring this heavenly food that is reserved in churches. This cult of adoration has a sound and firm foundation, especially since faith in the real presence of the Lord has as its usual consequence the outward, public manifestation of that belief' (ES 5)

C)   there is an essential link between the reserved sacrament and the Mass itself, which is at one and the same time and inseparably a sacrifice, a memorial of the death and resurrection of the Lord, and a sacred banquet. This link should be reflected in the physical and visual relationship between altar and tabernacle. In this way the faithful will be reminded that the presence of the Lord in the Blessed Sacrament derives from the celebration at the altar and is directed towards sacramental and spiritual communion (cf. ES 80)

D)   the Church greatly encourages devotion, both private and public, to the reserved sacrament. Such devotion is a public manifestation of the community's belief in the mystery of the eucharist (EM 49 & 58). 'Abiding with Christ the Lord they enjoy his intimate friendship and pour out their hearts before him for themselves and for those dear to them, and they pray for the peace and salvation of the world. Offering their entire lives with Christ to the Father in the Holy Spirit they derive from this sublime colloquy an increase of faith, hope and charity. Thus they foster those right dispositions that enable them with due devotion to celebrate the memorial of the Lord and receive frequently the bread given us by the Father' (ES 80).

The tabernacle: basic data

16.3 The tabernacle is a sacred receptacle in which the Blessed Sacrament is reserved.

16.4 There should be only one tabernacle in a church or oratory.

16.5 The tabernacle may be placed in a wall-niche or aumbry, on a pillar or in a eucharistic tower, or it may take the form of a hanging pyx. However, current legislation does not rule out other possible forms or developments.

16.6 The tabernacle should be dignified and properly ornamented with particular attention given to the design and decoration of the interior. It should be inviolable and made of solid non-transparent material. It should be lockable and secure against danger of profanation.

16.7 The reserved sacrament is kept in a pyx or ciborium in the tabernacle (GIRM 276-277; EM 52 & 57; CIC 938-940).

The tabernacle lamp

16.8 A special lamp is to burn continuously before the tabernacle in which the Blessed Sacrament is reserved, to indicate and honour the presence of Christ. According to traditional usage this takes the form of an oil lamp or a lamp with a wax candle (ES 11; CIC 940). The location and design of the lamp should be considered in conjunction with the location and design of the tabernacle so that there will be a proper relationship between them.

Design, setting and location of the tabernacle

16.9 The sacred character of the tabernacle can be expressed only by means of a true and contemplative art.

16.10 The location and design of the tabernacle and its setting should be determined in the light of the following principles:

A) The location of the tabernacle should be 'truly prominent' (EM 53), distinguished, conspicuous, suitably adorned and conducive to private contemplative prayer (CIC 938).

B) The location of the tabernacle should reflect the indissoluble relationship between the reserved sacrament and the Mass itself (cf. 16. 2c). The arrangement should be such, however, that the tabernacle does not dominate the altar or obscure its distinctive sign value as the place of banquet/sacrifice. Nor should the presence in the tabernacle overshadow the different forms of Christ's presence in the Mass, or obscure the way in which these gradually unfold: his presence in the assembled faithful, his presence in the word, his presence in the person of the presiding priest, and his presence substantially in the sacred species on the altar. On the other hand the tabernacle ought not be diminished or obscured by the altar. Each should be so treated and so related to the other that they will call attention to the distinct but inseparable aspects of the total eucharistic mystery (EM 3e, 50, 55).

C) The tabernacle in both design and setting should be in keeping with Christ's purpose in giving us this heavenly food: to nourish, heal and sustain us and to help us grow in communion with him and with one another (cf. EM 60).

D) The tabernacle should not be treated as subsidiary to any feature of its surroundings and should not therefore be surmounted by a throne or canopy for a monstrance or by display stands for a crucifix or flowers.

E) There should be a direct line of access between altar and tabernacle to provide for situations in which hosts have to be brought from the tabernacle for communion (in which case they should be first brought to the altar at the 'breaking of the bread'; however, care should be taken to enable the faithful to communicate with hosts consecrated during the Mass being celebrated (EM 31).

F) The location and design of the tabernacle and its setting should not only meet the needs and traditional devotion of people to the reserved sacrament but should facilitate a deepening of that devotion.

G) The location of the tabernacle should be such that it can be identified easily on entry to the church or from the main body of the church.

16.11 As with the other liturgical elements, the tabernacle should have its own distinctive location, visibly set apart for the purpose of reservation. Much more is therefore required than a merely arbitrarily chosen place, however convenient.

16.12 In deciding on the location of the tabernacle it is important to keep clearly in mind that there is no a priori 'best' location. Arrangements will vary in accordance with the particular circumstances of each church. In each instance careful study and discernment are required and serious efforts should be made by architects and artists, in cooperation with priests, to find creative ways of expressing eucharistic truth and of fostering eucharistic devotion through a sensitive treatment of space and atmosphere.

16.13 Two possible arrangements are recommended:

A: **A BLESSED SACRAMENT CHAPEL**

This arrangement is recommended by current legislation: 'It is highly recommended that the holy eucharist be reserved in a chapel suitable for private adoration and prayer' (GIRM 276). Such a setting can more easily provide an ambiance of quiet, calm and withdrawal, being of a scale conducive to intimate contemplative prayer and spiritual communion.

Should this arrangement be adopted, the following points should be borne in mind:

A) The chapel should be worthy of this great sacrament.

B) Its location should not obscure but rather emphasise the indissoluble relationship between the eucharistic celebration and the reserved eucharist (cf. 16:2c).

C) The chapel should not only meet the needs of the traditional devotion of people to the Blessed Sacrament but should deepen and foster it.

D) The chapel should be prominent, and not remote or closed off from the main body of the church.

E) The location of the chapel should be easily identifiable on entry to the church and from the main body of the church.

F) A location opening directly off the sanctuary can be particularly effective provided it does not result in two main focal points in the church.

G) The chapel should not have the appearance of being just one shrine among others.

H) The chapel should not be used for the celebration of Mass.

B: **THE TABERNACLE IN THE SANCTUARY**

This arrangement also accords with current legislation. A tabernacle in the sanctuary (but not on the altar), properly related to the altar and the other sanctuary elements, and visible to the congregation during Mass, public devotions and private prayer, can give a total, ordered and permanent unity to the whole church.

Being 'properly related to the altar' does not necessarily mean 'located in the centre behind the altar'. In fact, such an arrangement is not satisfactory from a liturgical point of view, as it can create its own problems by occasioning a visual tension between tabernacle and altar, since both are on the one axis; by requiring genuflections that disrupt liturgical movement and weaken recognition of Christ's presence in other forms (see 16:10b); and by drawing attention away from the progressive unfolding of Christ's presence during the celebration.

An arrangement in which the tabernacle is located in the sanctuary can maintain the relationship between the reserved sacrament and the Mass itself. If it is adopted the following should be observed:

A) The tabernacle should be dignified and properly ornamented.

B) The arrangement should be such as to foster private prayer.

C) The location of the tabernacle should not be such as to impede the full participation of the faithful in the eucharistic celebration nor diminish their understanding of it.

D) The tabernacle should not so dominate the altar as to obscure the distinctive doctrinal and liturgical sign value of the altar as the place of sacrifice, banquet and communion.

E) The tabernacle must not be located in an undefined space.

17 THE PLACE OF BAPTISM

(The Baptistry)

BAPTISM OF CHRIST, WEST CROSS, KELLS

The baptistry

17.1 The baptistry is the area which contains the baptismal font, or in which the baptismal water flows. The area should be reserved for the celebration of baptism and should be located and designed with the utmost care.

First of the sacraments of initiation

17.2 Baptism is the first of three sacraments by which a person is initiated into the people of God, the Church. It is 'the door to life and to the kingdom of God' (GICI 3).

   (In confirmation the baptised continue on their path of initiation, are enriched with the gift of the Spirit and are more closely linked with the Church. Finally, the baptised come to the table of the eucharist to join Christ in offering his sacrifice and to receive his body and blood in communion.)

17.3 The meaning and effects of baptism are expressed in its celebration through powerful images, mostly of a biblical nature: passage from darkness to light, from slavery to freedom, from blindness to vision, from death to life; dying and rising with Christ expressed through immersion in and emergence from water as from a tomb; washing and purification; destruction of the old within us, and rebirth; the stripping off of the old and the clothing in the new; creation and recreation; signings and anointings, vitality and growth.

Celebration

17.4 Normally baptism is to be celebrated in the presence of the baptised community and in a communal ceremony, i.e. involving more than one candidate.

In this way the faithful can show their common faith and express their joy as new members are incorporated into the Christian community.

17.5 The celebration of the sacrament for infants is carried out in four stages:

   A) reception of the infants with their parents and godparents by the minister and the community (preferably at the entrance to the church)

   B) liturgy of the word (preferably at the ambo)

   C) the liturgy of baptism (in the baptistry)

   D) concluding rites (at the altar)

17.6 Normally this will involve a number of processions of the baptismal party: from entrance to ambo, from ambo to font and from font to altar.

Location and design

17.7 The design of the place for each stage of the celebration of the sacrament requires consideration of the activities which occur at each place and of the relationship between them.

17.8 With the exception of the sanctuary and the space in which the Blessed Sacrament is reserved no area in the church is excluded as a possible location for the baptistry, provided the area is large enough to accommodate a good number of people, and provided the faithful can participate in the celebration of the sacrament.

   In this connection it may be noted that the entrance has a particular significance in relation to baptism, the first step in our 'entrance' or initiation into the people of God. Here the baptism of children or the admission of catechumens normally begins.

   It should be remembered that the ideal occasion for the celebration is the Paschal Vigil, that the celebration may take place occasionally at Sunday Mass, and that at other times too a large number of the faithful may be present. The location of the baptistry should facilitate the participation of the faithful on these occasions.

17.9 The baptismal area should be large enough to accommodate with ease the priest or deacon, the candidates, families, godparents, ministers and others who may be involved. The liturgy envisages the presence of 'the people of God, represented not only by the parents, godparents and relatives, but also as far as possible by friends, neighbours and some members of the local church' (GICI 7).

A font in every parish church

17.10 There is to be a baptistry with a baptismal font in all parish churches. Other churches or oratories will have these only if they have acquired the right already, or with the approval of the local Ordinary (CIC 858).

Immersion, infusion and their symbolism

17.11 The act of baptising with water should be given its full significance in the celebration of the sacrament. From what has been already indicated (17.2) it will be clear that baptism is much more than a rite of purification. Baptism may be carried out either by immersion in the water of the font or by infusion, i.e. pouring the water on the candidate's head over the font.

Suitability for adult baptism

17.12 The font should be designed in such a way that it is suitable for the baptism of adults as well as infants. It should be able to accommodate adults for baptism by immersion - at least by partial immersion. Even when it is not being used, the baptismal font should express something of the dignity and mystery of the sacrament.

Movable fonts should never be used, excepting the situation which can arise in the course of the Easter Vigil (cf. THE ROMAN MISSAL: THE EASTER VIGIL, 37).

Because of the possibility of immersion, consideration should be given to the provision of facilities for drying and dressing.

Forms of font

17.13 The font may take any of several different forms (with, e.g. moving 'living' water) and draw inspiration in its design from the rich symbolism associated with the waters of baptism.

If it can be done without obscuring the view of the font by those present at a baptism, a step or steps down to and up from the font may be provided as a means of expressing burial and resurrection with Christ.

The water

17.14 The water used in baptism should be clean, both because of its symbolism and for reasons of hygiene. Provision for heating the water should be made if necessary.

Seating

17.15 The provision of seating in the baptistry may be desirable, depending on the location of the baptistry, as a facility for those taking part in the ceremony.

Table, paschal candle stand, aumbry

17.16 It is desirable also to have a small table or surface in the baptistry to hold objects used in the celebration, e.g. the holy oils, books.

It is appropriate that a stand for the paschal candle (which is used in the celebration) be available in the baptistry.

An aumbry in the baptistry for the reservation of the holy oils can be a useful and attractive feature and an effective pedagogical aid.

The baptistry in a refurbished church

17.17 Where an existing church is to be adapted to meet the requirements of the liturgy the provision of a suitable baptistry must be considered at the same time. This may involve the construction of a new baptistry if the existing one, as is frequently the case, is in an obscure or restricted location.

18 THE PLACE OF RECONCILIATION

(The Confessional)

Terminology

18.1 The confessional is that place in the church where penitents individually confess their sins and are absolved in the sacrament of reconciliation.

The sacrament

18.2 The sacrament of reconciliation is a sacrament of loving welcome and forgiveness on the part of God, of sorrow and joyful return on the part of the penitent, and of reconciliation through and with the community of the Church. It is a personal encounter with Jesus Christ, through whose death and resurrection God has reconciled the world to himself and sent the Holy Spirit among us for the forgiveness of sins. It is a celebration, therefore, both of the mercy of God and of the joy of the penitent and the community.

All this should be reflected in the design of confessionals.

Location and design

18.3 By their design and location confessionals should manifest the dignity of the sacrament.

18.4 Confessionals should occupy an open, conspicuous area in the church, while at the same time being so designed that the secrecy of the penitent's confession is safeguarded.

18.5 Confessionals should reflect the role of the priest as the Church's minister of reconciliation and the communal as well as personal dimension of the sacrament (viz. that sin is sin against the community as well as against God, and reconciliation is reconciliation with the community as well as with God).

18.6 Confessionals need not necessarily be enclosed. It is possible by skilled design to establish a space or zone within the building which is clearly set apart for the celebration of the sacrament and in which the confidentiality and anonymity of the penitent can be respected.

18.7 Confessionals should be easily identifiable and accessible and they should be located in such a way that other activities which may be going on in the church at the same time will not constitute a disturbance.

18.8 The waiting area for penitents should be arranged so as to be conducive to the celebration of the sacrament and so that a dignified and orderly movement of people can be maintained, while any risk of confessions being overheard is averted.

18.9 Different areas of the church can be suitable for the location of confessionals. Thus, for example, a location near the church entrance makes access to the sacrament easier for some penitents.

18.10 Confessionals should have a hospitable ambience and evoke a friendly atmosphere. They should reflect the spirit of joy and celebration referred to above (18:2), a spirit which would not be facilitated by gloomy or austere surroundings.

Other requirements

18.11 The design of the confessional should take into account the requirement that the priest extend his hands, or at least his right hand, over the penitent's head during the words of absolution (OP 48). This gesture is an expression of the loving forgiveness of God mediated through Jesus Christ in the Spirit. It is a gesture of compassion, healing and reconciliation.

The strong recommendation that a passage of scripture be read by priest or penitent in the course of the celebration suggests the provision of a suitable book-rest or table which can be shared by both priest and penitent. The placing and display of the book can underline the importance of the word of God in the celebration.

Types of confessionals

18.12 It is difficult to envisage the traditional box-type confessionals as an adequate provision for the requirements of the Rite of Penance.

The room or open-space model of confessional can have the following advantages:

A) If properly designed it can provide the kind of ambiance called for by the Rite and facilitate its effective and reverent celebration.

B) It makes it possible for both priest and penitent to speak in a normal voice.

C) It facilitates the confession of handicapped and infirm penitents.

D) It makes possible the provision of better environmental conditions.

E) It allows more freedom to the confessor during intervals to make effective use of his time, e.g. in reading or writing.

Further aspects of design

18.13 The design of the confessional should express the following:

A) an atmosphere of welcome, repentance, reconciliation, encouragement, joy and celebration

B) an appreciation of the sacredness of the place in which the priest, in declaring and granting absolution, speaks in the name of the Trinity

C) an awareness that in this sacrament reconciliation takes place both with God and with the Church, 'our brothers and sisters who are always harmed by our sins' (OP 5)

D) a feeling of security and privacy without a sense of isolation or restraint

E) a sense of occasion, of an important activity, and not of a semi-automatic process

Additional facilities

18.14 In the design of the confessional areas consideration should be given to the provision of the following facilities:

A) a crucifix, visible to both priest and penitent

B) adequate sound insulation to safeguard privacy and to protect against any noise from without

C) equipment to assist those with impaired hearing

D) adequate space and accessibility for wheelchair occupants

E) some method of indicating that the confessional is occupied

F) an external bell push so that a confessor can be summoned (e.g. from sacristy or presbytery)

G) a reading light for the confessor, an extractor fan and a small heater

H) dimmer switches

I) reasonably comfortable seats and arm rests

Communal penance celebrations

18.15 In the design and arrangement of a church provision should be made also for the effective and worthy celebration of the Rite of Reconciliation of several penitents with individual Confession and Absolution ('RITE 2'). This rite envisages the possible presence of a large congregation of penitents, with more confessors than are generally provided for in the existing confessionals.

19 THE MORTUARY CHAPEL

Purpose

19.1   The provision of a mortuary chapel may be desirable, especially in smaller churches, where another service is liable to take place (e.g. a wedding) while a coffin is in the church.

The purpose of the mortuary chapel is not to provide for the funeral service but to provide a dignified place to which the coffin can be removed, when that is desirable, for a short period.

Design and location

19.2   In the design and decoration of the mortuary chapel there should be an emphasis on the relationship of death to baptism, to the paschal mystery (the passion, resurrection and return in glory of the Lord) and to the final resurrection from the dead. The chapel should be permeated with an atmosphere of Christian hope and faith.

19.3   If the altar cross cannot be clearly seen from the chapel a permanent cross should be provided.

19.4   The mortuary chapel can be located in any convenient place. For practical reasons care should be taken to provide adequate natural ventilation.

TOMB OF CHRIST, CROSS OF THE SCRIPTURES, CLONMACNOIS

20 IMAGES IN THE CHURCH

The function of images

20.1 The practice of placing images in churches for devotional reasons is a legitimate and commendable one. In the first place are images relating to the persons of the Blessed Trinity. Then there are images relating to the Blessed Virgin Mary and the saints. Special attention should be given to the mystery of salvation or the person to whom the church and the community were entrusted when the church was dedicated.

The veneration of the saints is primarily a proclamation of Jesus Christ and his paschal mystery.

> By celebrating the passage of these saints from earth to heaven the Church proclaims the paschal mystery achieved in the saints who have suffered and been glorified with Christ (SC 104).

Their place in the Church is further expressed in the Second Preface of Holy Men and Women in the Roman Missal:

> You renew the Church in every age
> by raising up men and women outstanding
>   in holiness,
> living witnesses of your unchanging love.
> They inspire us by their heroic lives,
> and help us by their constant prayers
> to be the living sign of your saving power
> (cf. SC 104 & LG 50).

BRONZE FIGURE OF ECCLESIASTIC, AGHABOE

The communion of saints

20.2 The treatment of images in any part of the church should express the reality of the communion of saints and the participation of the congregation in the heavenly liturgy (SC 8). The intimate relationship of the saints to the liturgy is emphasised by the references to them in the eucharistic prayers of the Mass. Their part in the communion of saints is similarly emphasised, thereby indicating their close ties with Christians on earth both as individuals and as the people of God.

These relationships are expressed and encouraged by the provision of suitable images within the church.

Christian images

20.3 Authentic Christian images do not merely portray the persons represented or the events of salvation. Neither are they merely reminders of the virtues of the saints. It is their aim to evoke the intuition that the Lord is present in his Church, that already we enjoy communion with the saints as a foretaste of eventual union with them in the kingdom, that the mysteries of salvation history give meaning and orientation to our lives, and that the glory promised us transfigures our existence even now (cf. DS 11).

20.4 Images are specifically Christian when they are linked to the paschal mystery. The true Christian image can speak either directly or symbolically. The 'cult image' relates to and has its place in liturgical celebration; its primary expression is the icon. The 'devotional image' relates to private prayer and popular devotion. The Church has place for both.

Retaining works of art

20.5 Where existing images which are genuine works of art are available it can be desirable to use them. Such use can reinforce local tradition. But the setting of the image requires careful consideration so that it does not suggest that it is a museum or gallery exhibit.

Location of images

20.6 It is desirable that each image have its own place designed for it, so that

> A) its intrinsic importance is expressed by the dignity of the setting;
>
> B) the private devotion of the faithful is facilitated;
>
> C) the architectural character of the building is enhanced rather than diminished.

Uncontrolled multiplication or haphazard location of images may devalue true devotion and should be avoided. In particular, crosses should not be multiplied or used merely for decorative purposes.

Images of Mary

20.7 Every church should contain an image of the Blessed Virgin Mary. As well as expressing her singular place in the liturgy, the location of her image should allow for personal devotion. This location should be determined as early as possible within the context of the overall design of the church. An appropriate setting for the image, which could be in a special space, or chapel, ought to be provided.

The Way of the Cross

20.8 Treatment of images for the Way of the Cross makes a considerable demand on the artist's skill if it is to recall effectively the passion of Christ and yet infuse the work with a sense of resurrection, joy and triumph. Sometimes it may help to associate images through colour, form, material and treatment with the sanctuary cross and its theme of death, resurrection and ascension. The images should not, either by size or colouring, dominate the interior of the church. Space should be allowed for movement, at least of the person leading the prayers, between the stations.

Temporary use of images

20.9 When images are introduced for a temporary period, e.g. during the great seasons of Advent, Christmas, Lent, Easter or during a novena, they should comply with the foregoing directives. A lower standard should not be acceptable merely because the image is to be displayed only for a short period.

Shrines

20.10 A shrine is a place set apart within or outside a church to contain an image or some object of devotion such as a relic. It is desirable that shrines should not be haphazardly located around a church but should be planned in carefully defined relationship to the architectural framework of the building. The decoration of a shrine should be related and subordinate to the object enshrined, but at the same time it should have an appropriate richness sufficient to indicate the importance of that object.

21 SACRED VESSELS

Materials and functional requirements

21.1   Sacred vessels are necessary for the celebration of the liturgy. Among these the chalice and paten are particularly important because of the function they serve.

21.2   Sacred vessels should be fashioned from durable materials. If a metal which oxidises (e.g. copper) is used it should be gilded on the interior surface. Gilding is not otherwise required, unless it is required by the nature of the design.

21.3   Vessels may be made of any valuable and appropriate material, but chalices must have a cup of non-absorbent material.

21.4   There is no restriction, other than those of functional requirements, on the shape or decoration of sacred vessels, but because of their particular importance they should always be designed by an artist.

21.5   The principles set out above will apply in some instances to vessels or receptacles which are used for liturgical, sacramental or devotional purposes outside Mass.

DERRYNAFLAN STRAINER

22 VESTMENTS

Rubrical requirements

22.1 In celebrating and administering the eucharist priests and deacons are to wear the sacred vestments prescribed by the rubrics (CIC 929).

22.2 Not all the members of the liturgical assembly have the same function to perform. In the course of a celebration the different ministries which are carried out are indicated by the use of different vestments. As well as signifying the role proper to each minister, vestments help to make the ceremonies beautiful, solemn and festive.

Materials and design

22.3 In addition to traditional materials, vestments may be made from natural fabrics of the region or artificial fabrics in keeping with the dignity of the sacred action and of the person wearing them.

22.4 The beauty of a vestment should derive from its material and form rather than from its ornamentation. If images or symbols are used they should be in keeping with the function of the vestment. The form and cut of the vestments should be such that they hang freely and with dignity. As far as possible vestments should be designed in such a way that they harmonise with the ambience of the particular church in which they are used.

22.5 The design of vestments should be entrusted to a competent artist.

Colours

22.6 Colours in vestments give an effective expression to the celebration of the mysteries of the faith and in the course of the year create a sense of progress in the Christian life.

CRUCIFIXION PLAQUE FROM CLONMACNOIS

Altar ministers

22.7 Where the tradition of vested altar servers is maintained it is desirable that they wear a standard form of vestment, preferably the alb.

23 CANDLES AND LAMPS

23.1 'Candles are required during liturgical services to express devotion or the degree of festivity. They should be placed either on the altar or around it' (GIRM 269).

All candleholders should be specially designed and unobtrusive. They should be removed when not in use. The candleholder for the paschal candle should be designed by an artist to express its singular liturgical significance.

23.2 Candles and oil lamps with their living flame are symbols of the risen Christ. They are reminders of our transformation from darkness to light in baptism.

The use of souches or metal tubes to encase candles, or the use of imitation candles or imitation votive lamps, frustrates the symbolism of candles; they are not permitted for Mass or for other liturgical services.

The paschal candle

23.3 'The paschal candle has its proper place either by the ambo or by the altar, and should be lit at least in all the more solemn liturgical celebrations of the season [of Easter] until Pentecost Sunday, whether at Mass or at Morning and Evening Prayer. After the Easter Season the candle should be kept with honour in the baptistry, so that in the celebration of baptism the candles of the baptised may be lit from it. In the celebration of funerals the paschal candle should be placed near the coffin to indicate that death is the Christian's passover. The paschal candle should not, otherwise, be lit nor placed in the sanctuary outside the Easter season' (CIRCULAR LETTER OF THE CONGREGATION FOR DIVINE WORSHIP ON THE PREPARATION AND CELEBRATION OF THE EASTER FEASTS, 16 JANUARY 1988, NO. 98).

Votive lamps and candles

23.4 The practice of lighting candles before images is to be encouraged but the design of candle-holders should be such that they form an integral part of the shrine. Artificial lighting of votive lamps is unacceptable, and the use of electricity for such cultic purposes as votive lamps, haloes, etc., is to be altogether avoided.

23.5 Risks of fire and of personal injury should be taken into account in the design and location of shrines. Such dangers can be greatly reduced if the design and location are planned with care.

23.6 Lamps should not be given excessive emphasis and should not obscure the view of the altar, tabernacle or sanctuary cross. They may be hanging or standing or fixed to a wall. Old sanctuary lamps, if of good design and workmanship, can be incorporated into a renovation project when they are suitable for their locations.

24 FLOWERS AND PLANTS

24.1 Flowers and plants may be used as an adornment but any effect of crowding or over-decoration must be avoided. Emphasis should be placed on the grouping of plants rather than on isolated, sometimes distracting, flower arrangements or arches. Artificial flowers or branches, or other such ornaments, may never be used within churches.

24.2 Containers for flowers should be well designed in relation to their surroundings. Containers should be removed as soon as the occasion for the use of the flowers or plants has ceased.

24.3 Arrangements of flowers or plants should never obscure the liturgical integrity and symbolism of the altar, ambo or chair. A small arrangement of flowers discreetly placed on the altar may be acceptable.

24.4 The use of plants is appropriate in the vicinity of the tabernacle, the baptismal font and the mortuary chapel.

CARNDONAGH CROSS-PILLAR, LITURGICAL FAN WITH MARIGOLD PATTERN (TOP)

25 THE FOUNDATION STONE

25.1 When the building of a new church begins, it is customary to celebrate a rite to ask God's blessing on the work which is to be undertaken. In accordance with liturgical tradition this rite consists in the blessing of the site of the new church and the blessing and laying of the foundation stone.

25.2 In so far as possible, the area which the church will occupy should be well marked out. It should be possible to walk around it conveniently.

25.3 In the place where the altar will be located a wooden cross of appropriate height should be placed.

25.4 For the celebration of the rite the following should be prepared:

A) the foundation stone, which is traditionally a corner-stone and rectangular, together with cement and the tools for placing the stone in the foundation

B) speaking equipment, so that the assembly may clearly hear the readings, prayers and instructions.

25.5 A document on durable material, using permanent ink, recording the blessing of the foundation stone and the commencement of the building of the church should be prepared. It is signed by the bishop and by the representatives of those who are going to work on the building of the church, and, having been encased in an airtight box, it is enclosed together with the stone in the foundations.

25.6 When he has finished the blessing the bishop lays the stone on the foundations in silence. A stonemason then fixes the stone in place with mortar.

25.7 The foundation stone should be designed as to type, size and layout of lettering by an artist.

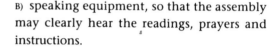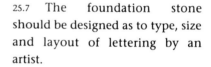

FOUNDATION OF CLONMACNOIS WITH ST CIARAN AND DERMOT, CROSS OF THE SCRIPTURES, CLONMACNOIS

26 ORATORIES AND PRIVATE CHAPELS

26.1 An oratory is   place which, by permission of the Ordinary, is s   ide for divine worship for the convenience of some community or group which assembles there, to which, however, other members of the faithful may, with the consent of the competent superior, have access (CIC 1223).

A private chapel is a place which, by permission of the local Ordinary, is set aside for divine worship for the convenience of one or more individuals (CIC 1226).

Design factors and principles

26.2 The arrangement and decoration of the space and the provision of furnishings should be done in accordance with a carefully prepared overall design. The fact that the space may be small does not dispense from the necessity f uch a design. Special attention should be paid both to the character of the group or the persons who will use the oratory or private chapel and to the range of liturgical functions normally to be celebrated there.

26.3 The basic principles enunciated in this Directory and enshrined in its provisions with regard to churches apply also in the case of oratories and private chapels. In particular, those principles which concern the liturgical assembly, the relationship of priest and people, the arrangements of the elements of the sanctuary, and the placing of the people must be respected.

Sense of unity

26.4 In general the smaller size of oratories and private chapels and the fact that they will not generally be used for the full range of liturgical services should make possible a greater sense of unity in the celebration of the liturgy and a more intimate atmosphere in private prayer. This should also allow for a greater measure of flexibility in the spatial relationship of priest and people. This relationship involves both unity and differentiation of role in the liturgical assembly. The type of seating used and the arrangement of the seating should be given careful consideration in the light of these possibilities.

The elements

26.5 The altar, the ambo and the chair should be provided for and designed in accordance with the principles given earlier in this Directory, and the relationship between these should be respected, with ample space for the normal liturgical movements. However, if the space available is very small, it may not be possible to accommodate all these in a fitting manner. In this case it would be better to omit the ambo than to provide an unworthy object or to clutter the sanctuary excessively.

Tabernacle

26.6 If the Blessed Sacrament is to be reserved in a small oratory or private chapel special care will be needed in locating and designing the tabernacle. The principles which apply to the location and design of the tabernacle in the case of churches (see Chapter 16) apply also in this case.

26.7 It should be noted that in a house of a religious institute or other houses of piety the Blessed Sacrament is to be reserved only in the church or principal oratory attached to the house; it may be reserved also in another oratory of the same house only with the permission of the Ordinary, given for a just reason (CIC 936).

Altar, a necessary element

26.8 In such cases there should always be an altar, where Mass is celebrated at least on occasion. The presence of the altar expresses the relationship between the reserved sacrament and the Mass, and is a reminder that the reserved sacrament derives from the Mass and leads to sacramental and spiritual communion.

Blessing

26.9 It is fitting that oratories and private chapels be blessed (cf. ODEA 5 & CIC 1229).

GALLARUS ORATORY

27 THE REORDERING AND ADAPTATION OF CHURCHES, ORATORIES AND OTHER PLACES OF WORSHIP

27.1 The principles set out in this Directory apply equally to new and existing places of worship.

Need for an overall plan

27.2 All renovation work should be planned against the overall background of a total renovation project, even if the work is to be carried out in stages over a period of years. Each stage of the work should be successful in itself; moreover, it should not inhibit any work at a later stage. The preliminary design, therefore, should envisage all work to be carried out eventually.

27.3 All such projects no matter how small should be carried out under the direction of an architect in close cooperation with an artist or artists, selected on the basis of their sensitive understanding of the character of the existing church.

Assessment and conservation

27.4 At times there may be a conflict between the requirements of the liturgy and the desire to conserve existing buildings of merit. If the building is of particular architectural, historical or social merit the reordering should be in sympathy with the character and detail of the building, while at the same time providing that effective liturgical environment which must always be the primary consideration.

27.5 The assessment of the character and quality of a building is of fundamental importance. The appropriate diocesan commissions should always be consulted and the advice of experts in architecture, history and the arts obtained before decisions are made. In all cases the matter must be referred to the Ordinary for a decision.

Records

27.6 Before work commences a complete record in the form of measured drawings and photographs should be made and kept in a secure archive.

Alterations not to be in isolation

27.7 The reordering of a church is not just a matter of alterations to a sanctuary. The sanctuary cannot be considered in isolation from the context of the entire worship space. Still less is reordering a matter of making minimal alterations so as to cater for 'Mass facing the people'. The objective is to create spaces in which the meaning and importance of the different moments of the liturgy will be evident from the location and design of the elements. The further objective is to provide spaces sufficiently large and proportioned as to provide for a dignified and meaningful carrying out of movements, processions and other activities relating to the liturgy.

Removal or adaptation of elements

27.8 To remove existing elements (altar, reredos, font, pulpit, etc.), some of which were admired and loved, most of which were at least familiar and accepted, and some of which were erected in memory of generous donors, is a decision which will require careful and sensitive handling.

27.9 Some such elements are genuine works of art. Occasionally there may be found in existing churches works of genuine merit or historical value. Destruction or mutilation of such would be inadmissible. However, because of historical circumstances, it is unusual to find such objects in Irish churches. Many are not of genuine artistic value, however imposing in size or decoration they may be. Frequently they were selected by the client from the studios of commercial firms, ready-made and without adequate reference to the particular church and its furnishings. In the reordering of a worship space their retention can make the planning of proper liturgical space very difficult.

Adaptation of altars

27.10 It must be emphasised that the mere moving forward of the table of an existing altar while leaving the tabernacle set in an existing reredos almost never produces a satisfactory solution (cf. 14.10).

Consultation with experts

27.11 Where the reordering and adaptation is being carried out in a church of special historical or artistic merit, the advice of experts should be sought in relation to the preservation and conservation of the building and its distinctive features (cf. TI 10).

27.12 Advice should also be sought regarding the quality and artistic merit of works proposed for removal or adaptation. If the advice is that the element is a genuine work of art, attempts to adapt it are unlikely to be successful. Its artistic merit and beauty may depend on its being retained as a single piece. For example, the separation of an altar from a reredos may gravely damage the artistic quality of both.

27.13 As a general rule, therefore, existing elements should be either retained completely or removed completely. Adaptation may, however, be a possibility in the hands of competent architects and artists, whose skill may be able both to preserve the artistic value of the element and to create a fitting liturgical environment.

27.14 Artistic quality is not, of course, the only relevant consideration. There may be other reasons why it is felt that an existing element should be retained. In such a case, too, expert advice should be sought.

27.15 Both the artistic quality and the intrinsic financial value of elements (particularly altars) are often overestimated. In many cases the marble content is only a facade on a brick or concrete interior; and the actual marble used is often low-grade. The expense of dismantling and remounting is considerable and the result will be a hybrid, neither old or new. The pleasing qualities of the original came from the unity between its parts. When this is broken there is no longer either whatever beauty the past had or the beauty the present needs.

Unwarranted alterations and additions

27.16 It sometimes happens that subsequent alterations and additions are made to churches, both new and refurbished, which have been designed in a competent and coordinated way according to this Directory. If such alterations and additions are made without the advice of the original designer or of another expert in the field there is a grave risk of impairing the quality and liturgical appropriateness of the worship space. Any additional items or alterations no matter how small (e.g. painting the church) should be carried out only under the direction of an artist and/or architect.

27.17 Examples of undesirable alterations would be
- resiting of the tabernacle
- changes in location or design of liturgical elements
- the provision of lecterns at the president's chair
- superfluous floral arrangements
- images and permanent banners

- chairs and kneelers for altar servers
- the replacement of crucifixes, statues and images which were the work of artists of repute with substitutes of inferior quality

Such actions are arbitrary and unjustifiable.

27.18 If, when a reasonable period has elapsed following the building or reordering of a church or the erection of some work of art in a place of worship, questions are raised about the quality or acceptability of a particular work, the matter should be referred to the local Ordinary or to whatever body he has appointed to act on his behalf (such as the diocesan Commission on Art and Architecture). In addition, the architects and artists originally involved should normally be consulted, with a view to arriving at a fully informed decision before any alterations are undertaken.

Disposal of liturgical and devotional objects

27.19 In the liturgical renewal of recent years many items of liturgical and devotional use have been withdrawn from use. Priests should take care in the conservation or eventual disposal of such objects, which have served a holy purpose.

27.20 From time to time objects used in the celebration of the liturgy or in devotional practices may deteriorate or may be superseded by others of better design or may become superfluous, and it may be necessary to withdraw them. When this happens, great care should be taken in deciding what is to be done.

27.21 An assessment of each object should be made by an expert so as to determine if it is a work of artistic value. 'Ordinaries should ensure that sacred furnishings and works of value are not disposed of or destroyed, for they are ornaments of God's house' (sc 126). If the work, even though it may have an appreciable monetary value, possesses no artistic value it should be withdrawn from use.

27.22 Where the object has been blessed or consecrated (e.g. altars, sacred vessels) it must under no circumstances be sold or given away if there is any possibility, however remote, of its being put to any unworthy use. The disposal of all such objects must be submitted to the judgement of the local Ordinary, who will decide whether they may be sold or given away, and to whom. If he should decide against a sale or gift the object must be deposited and maintained carefully and reverently in a secure place, preferably in a diocesan or public museum.

27.23 Objects which have not been blessed or consecrated but have been used for the purpose of liturgy or devotion may not be sold or given away except for use in some other church, oratory or Catholic institution or society, without the specific permission of the Ordinary. They may be disposed of by being destroyed (preferably by fire).

27.24 A particular object may be of some pastoral worth, being sincerely revered by many members of the community, even though it may possess no other value. In such a case, it should be replaced by a better object and it would be desirable to accompany the replacement by an explanation which draws attention to the positive value of the new object.

27.25 Other objects of church furnishing (e.g. seating - other than the presidential chair) may be disposed of in any appropriate manner.

28 **DISUSED CHURCHES**

28.1   Careful thought should be given to the question of the future of disused churches. They enshrine the memories of the local community and have been consecrated by long use and the prayers of generations.

28.2   Such buildings should not be allowed to become hazardous or to be used for any unworthy purpose. They should be treated with sensitivity and if possible converted to some fitting and worthy use, e.g. a parish hall or museum. If it should be necessary to demolish an old church, some mark and evidence of its former use should be retained.

28.3   The ultimate decision regarding the future of disused churches rests with the local Ordinary.

Appendix 1

BUILDING MAINTENANCE

Appendix 2

SOME RESOURCE MATERIAL

It is not sufficient to achieve a well designed and constructed environment for the liturgy and then to allow it to deteriorate and become unattractive through lack of maintenance of the building. It is essential that maintenance should be carried out on a regular and methodical basis (a suitable basis is set out in the Maintenance Manual which is available from the Irish Institute of Pastoral Liturgy, College Street, Carlow, while useful sources of information as to the investigation of defects and remedial work are available in the *Building Digests, Information Papers* and *Defect Action Sheets* published by the Building Research Establishment, Garston, Watford WD2 7JR, England). Many useful booklets have been published by the Council for the Care of Churches (Church of England), 83 London Wall, London EC2M 5NA

Sacrosanctum Concilium, the Constitution on the Sacred Liturgy, the first document from the Second Vatican Council, was promulgated on 4 December 1963. It is regarded as the charter for a renewal of the Church's worship in which the 'full and active participation of all the people [would be] the aim to be considered before all else' (*SC* 14). Its seventh chapter is on sacred art and sacred furnishings. The *Constitution* remains the inspiration for a renewed understanding of the worship space and its elements and furnishings.

Each of the revised liturgical books, issued in the light of *Sacrosanctum Concilium,* has its own specific contribution to make. Of special note are the *General Instruction of the Roman Missal,* in particular chapter V: arrangements and furnishing of churches for the eucharistic celebration, and chapter VI: requisites for celebrating Mass, and the *Rite of Dedication of a Church and an Altar.* The prayers, readings and actions of the liturgical rites express the meaning of the Church's worship. The introductions or praenotanda of the liturgical books, many mentioned in this Directory, are important summaries of the Church's understanding of its worship and of the implications of this for art and architecture in the variety of liturgical services. They are a most valuable resource.

Many of these documents may be found in Austin Flannery, OP (ed.), *Vatican Council II: Conciliar and Postconciliar Documents,* 2 vols. (Dublin, Dominican Publications, 1975/1992), in *Documents of the Liturgy 1963-1979; Conciliar, Papal and Curial Texts* (Collegeville, Liturgical Press, 1982) and in Mark G. Boyer, *The Liturgical Environment, What the Documents Say* (Collegeville, Liturgical Press, 1990).

Two national directories should be noted:

Environment and Art in Catholic Worship, statement of the United States Catholic Conference (1977) and *The Parish Church: Principles of Liturgical Design and Reordering*, from the Bishops' Conference of England and Wales (1983).

Among the several good introductions to our renewed understanding of worship are: A. G. Martimort (ed.), *The Church at Prayer*, in four volumes: principles of the liturgy, the eucharist, the sacraments, the liturgy and time (London, Geoffrey Chapman, 1986-88); J. G. Davies (ed.), *A New Dictionary of Liturgy and Worship* (London, SCM Press, 1986); Peter E. Fink, SJ (ed.), *The New Dictionary of Sacramental Worship* (Dublin, Gill & Macmillan, 1990) and Cheslyn Jones, Geoffrey Wainwright, Edward Yarnold, SJ and Paul Bradshaw (eds.) *The Study of Liturgy* (London, SPCK, 1992).

Aspects of art and architecture are treated in many of these books as well as in others dealing specifically with these matters. Earlier works include Frederick Debuyst, *Modern Architecture and Christian Celebration* (London, Lutterworth Press, 1968); Rudolf Schwartz, *The Church Incarnate* (Chicago, Henry Regnery Co., 1958); J. G. Davies, *The Architectural Setting of Baptism* (London, Barrie & Rockliff, 1962); Peter Hammond, *Liturgy and Architecture* (London, Barrie & Rockliff, 1960) and Peter Hammond (ed.), *Towards a Church Architecture* (London, Architectural Press, 1962).

A study of church developments in Ireland, featuring forty churches built since 1937, is available in Richard Hurley and Wilfrid Cantwell, *Contemporary Irish Church Architecture* (Dublin, Gill & Macmillan, 1985). This book also contains a valuable introduction by Austin Flannery, OP.

Liturgy Training Publications, Chicago have several helpful studies including Marchita Mauck, *Shaping a House for the Church* (1990); Regina Kuehn, *A Place for Baptism* (1992) and Bill Brown (ed.), *Building and Renovation Kit for Places of Catholic Worship* (1982).

Among periodicals there are: *Notitiae*, the monthly bulletin of the Congregation for Divine Worship (Libreria Editrice Vaticana, Città del Vaticano); *New Liturgy*, quarterly bulletin of the national secretariat, Irish Episcopal Commission for Liturgy (Irish Institute of Pastoral Liturgy, Carlow); *Liturgy*, bi-monthly review from the Liturgy Office, Bishops' Conference of England and Wales (39 Eccleston Square, London SW1V 1PL); *Church Building* (quarterly, Gabriel Communications, St James's Buildings, Oxford St, Manchester M1 6FP); *Environment and Art Letter: a forum on architecture and the arts for the parish* (monthly, Liturgy Training Publications, Chicago); *Chroniques d'Art Sacré*, quarterly bulletin from the Centre National de Pastorale Liturgique (4 av. Vavin, 75007 Paris) and *Worship* (bi-monthly, Liturgical Press, Collegeville).

The list of these publications is not intended to be comprehensive or even to identify all those works which are of particular importance or value; its purpose is to indicate some basic reading for those involved in the practical problems of church design whether for new buildings or the renovation of existing buildings.

INDEX

reference to chapter/paragraph